The Writer's Craft:

My 13 Steps to Publishing

By DC Brownlow

Conant Gardens Publishing

Detroit, MI 48212

The Writer's Craft: My 13 Steps to Publishing

By DC Brownlow

Printed in the United States of America.
This book is printed on acid-free paper

Title: The Writing Craft: My13 Steps

ISBN 978-0-9828603-0-4

CONANT GARDENS PUBLISHING CO.

Detroit Michigan 48212
United States

www.conantgardens.com

The Writer's Craft:

My 13 Steps to Publishing

By DC Brownlow

Other Books by Christina Reyes:

**The Passing of Mother Mary

**From Michigan Maine to Harvard

Dedication

This book is dedicated to all those who find writing a difficult task and yearn for an easier way to expose their writing craft.

DON'T SAY IT ANYMORE...JUST DO IT!

"It will clear up some confusion and explain the publishing process for the novice writer." - **Autumn J. Conley, Book Editor**

Contents

OVERVIEW

WRITING THE NOVEL

(INTRO STEPS for the Novice or first-time **Writer)**

1. **Writing a novel**

2. **Copyright**

3. **ISBN**

4. **BARCODES**

5. **Editing**

6. **Proofreading**

7. **Cover Design**

8. **Printing Interior**

9. **Order Books**

10. **Marketing**

11. **Press Releases**

12. **Book Tours**

13. **Website(s)**

WRITING THE NOVEL

Each Author has their own story as to how they've walked the long road of their Writer's Craft I am no exception. My approach is my approach, and yours may be totally different. I am only an expert in this area because of the steps I took. Your journey on the writing road may be much different from mine. It is what it is. This book is not a Bible for writers—only a guided tour of my experiences as a Dyslexic who became a Writer and was told, "If you can't, then don't worry, for you are not alone." I will not tell you that. I will tell you, "Just do it!" Why? Because I did it, and I'm Dyslexic! And now, I am a Writer and a Published Author!

I've always had so many stories stored in my mind's eye, and they wanted a release. If I could spread some bit of encouragement to you all about how to follow and accomplish Writing and Publishing with a leap of faith, then I have will have traversed a second mountain. Having authored two books, and now this one and others to follow, I am reaching the greatest heights I've ever wanted to climb to and now you must do the same. I only ask that afterwards, you, too, will stretch out your hand and help someone else climb similar mountains. You must! I believe all writers and authors should take a cumulative effort to help others write and publish as someone was there to help them. Whatever you want to call it—passing the baton, paying it forward, mentoring someone else—I ask that you will do as I am doing.

Good luck to all of you writers. I know I will see your book(s) on the shelves.

~ DC Brownlow

DC BROWNLOW'S

Writing and Publishing Steps

Check off these steps as you complete them. Most of them can be done in the order here, but you can also do them in the order of importance as you see it. I will focus and discuss the importance of your manuscript or your story in my order of steps. The publishing steps will follow. This list below is the order in which I completed my books:

1. **Manuscript:** Completed.

2. **Copyright the Manuscript:** I would do this before editing, unless you trust your editor explicitly.

3. **ISBN/Barcode for the Manuscript:** Get this if you really want the book to be Yours! The Publisher(s) will sell you one of their ISBN numbers at a cheaper price, but they own the book, not your story! Booksellers will go to the Publisher to

purchase copies of your book, and you just have to hope your book gets to the bookstores and sellers. That's a lot of trust, ya know.

4. **Editing the Manuscript:** To some people, this is an absolute must. As a Dyslexic, I chose to find an editor. This is not a bad idea, and can prove very useful.

5. **Proofreading X 2:** Let an avid Reader do this part, not just your family and friends who will just support your efforts no matter what. I know this is your dream, so write regardless of what your readers may think, but run it past a second set of eyes for a good polish.

6. **PDF of Manuscript:** Make a PDF file document. You will need this to prevent any kind of malicious changes or misrepresentation, send to printers, and load your book on some eBook websites.

7. **PDF of Cover:** Make a PDF file document of the cover as well. Again, this will

prevent malicious changes to your cover art and you will need it if you want to send your book to publishers and/or printers or upload it on some eBook sites.

8. **Publisher(s)/Printer(s)** You make the decision to send to a publisher or printer. If you choose the publishing method, you pay the publisher to complete the publishing process, by having their printing companies print your book. With the printer option, you decide the printing company and mediate their prices; you chose the quantity of books and the quality of paper and book cover(s) used.

9. **Distribution:** Find a distribution company if you are self-publishing. If you are going through a publisher, the publisher will provide and do the contacting of these distribution companies, so they can have your book(s) readily ordered and sent to booksellers and stores for retail sale.

10. **Book Promotion:** You have to decide how to effectively promote your book. Some suggestions I would consider, are press releases, bookmarks, flyers, business cards, press kits, and book trailers. You can ask for and provide book reviews, advertisements, banners, various kinds of book displays, and miscellaneous items to display your book to the public.

11. **Book Signing(s)/Release Party:** You just finished you story after months of writing and went through all the pre-publishing and publishing steps. Why not celebrate? Book signings and a release party can really get the word out about your book, and then you can move on to the hardest part: international fame!

12. **Query Letter(s):** Now it's okay to write a query letter. In order to find that one agent to invest in your efforts, dreams, goals of being an accomplished and career author, it takes time and patience which is why it is good to have a published book

rather than a draft; agents will not take you seriously as a writer until you can show them a completed project.

13. **Share your FAME:** Tell other would-be writers how you did it. Your advice won't be the Bible to the Writer's Craft, just your own unique experience that will enable you to offer guidance.

Now, do you have your shoes on? Good! Let's walk through these steps the way I think it is best to focus on them. Let's climb the writer's mountain! Follow me and let's write and publish your books in 13 steps!

Why Do I Write?

People ask me all the time why I write. Well, I've thought about it and thought about it, and all I have to say is, why not? All the words in the world will not make my readers fully understand why I, the writer, engage in writing short stories, poems, and novels. Yet I am a writer. As most writers would say, I love what I write. I like telling a good tale. I like entertaining myself with a good story. I like putting myself in an unimaginable world of conflict, turmoil, or even settling in a utopian society. If it's good to me, I keep going.

My talent started at an early age. I was the unusual child in the family—the "strange" one. I remember being in the basement of my grandmother's house, talking to myself, not necessarily mentally, but creatively. I told stories to my dolls and stuffed animals. Neither my two sisters nor my mother were as interested in my tales, and a lonely child resorts to creative ways of unleashing their bottled-up thoughts and ideas. Even now, the images in my mind need freedom; like a bird, they'd rather fly than be stuck in a cage. The wind of ideas must feel itself flowing about without apprehension.

I like words, even though some people don't. Many readers (and some writers) often shy away from dictionaries or thesauruses. I have Dyslexia, so words don't jump off the page or come easily to my mind. They get scrambled sometimes like a literary omelet in my head. Yes, it bothers me, but I will not allow that to hinder my progress or intimidate me into putting down my pen. I am only human, and I realize I have limitations. But I know what those limitations are, and I won't allow this twitch of the particles in my brain to become an excuse not to Write. I consider myself a female soldier, and I can 'will' my way to conquering any obstacle.

My first book was *Betsy and Billy*. I fell in love with those two kids. My young mind wanted to possess a good book. As writers, we sometimes steal ideas and thoughts from others and the creativity in our own minds and place those stolen ideas on paper. When I entered junior high school (they call it middle school now), I was able to fill my own library thanks to Scholastic Book Clubs. That did it for me! I was immediately hooked on entering the world of others; the diverse worlds of authors and their characters. I read and read and read book after book after book. I couldn't stop. Reading was like a crack pipe, and I became addicted. I took books everywhere: to the doctor's office, to my dentist appointments, and on our family trips to Canada and New York. I was addicted to ink on paper, to the worlds, the lives, the feelings, and the thoughts lying beneath the words on the page,

When I entered high school, I had to write, and my language arts and creative writing classes were no joke. We wrote daily: paragraphs, journals, different kinds of essays and yes, creative stories. Even a simple paragraph was very challenging, especially for me. My creative writing teacher once asked me to read one of my narrative essays aloud, and I hated it. In addition to my dyslexia, I'd always suffered from stuttering and reading difficulties. I was already considered Dyslexic, so I wondered why she would make me read aloud. After several refusals, I confronted this teacher in a fit of anger.

The teacher, of course, told me what I did not want to hear: "You write so well that I just want others to hear your words. Don't let your talents be limited by what you can't control. God gives us all we need to survive. You can control your Dyslexia and stuttering with persistence and determination."

Yes, I needed inspiration. Everyone does. Some people need that one person that can tell them to take a deep breath, exhale, and then move forward without hesitation. At home, there was only one inspiration. My grandma Talley read one of my unfinished stories that she found in a drawer and asked why I hadn't finished it. It was science fiction, outside my genre of choice. I'm an avid Stephen King reader, but I can't write horror or suspense stories like him. He has his own creative style, and I have mine. But my grandmother really like the story I had drafted. That particular moment was so important to me; it changed my life to know that someone in my household finally took noticed of something I did... and obviously did well! Grandma Talley often said to me, "You are better than you think, baby."

I wrote for years prior to getting published, sometimes for therapy and sometimes for pure entertainment. To transport your life and your thoughts into words on a page is very therapeutic, but it can be a waste of talent for a writer if you are seeking acknowledgement for your craft. If you like to be entertained, entertain yourself before others. Self-gratification is a good thing! If you cannot please yourself in what you do, how can you expect others to be pleased?

So, why do I write? Therapy? Entertainment? Talent? Maybe it's just because it's something I can do creatively. Whatever my reason is, I know it is something I do well, and I will not let another day go by without telling a new tale, without giving the world a part of me. In me, God has created a creative being. He has given me and built within me something special. He has seen my potential. You have potential as well, so follow my inspiration. Dream with me, write with me, and express your talents with me. If not for the fun of it, just to entertain yourself, since you are the most important person you know.

Why do I write? Because I Can.

Journal:

Why Do You Write?

(Use this page to examine yourself and make your own list of the things that motivate you to write. I have included some examples to get you started.)

1.   I like to daydream about a world outside of my own.

2.   I like to tell good tales.

3.

4.

5.

6.

7.

8.

9.

10.

The Breakdown

Now I will break down the steps so the novice and newest writers will understand the publishing process explicitly. The order on the "overview page" will be explained, but in a new order. It is the same climb; my 13 steps to climbing the mountain of Writing and Publishing. I have been asked to give many seminars on my Publishing process, and this lecture is actually being explained here.

So sit back in your conference seat and listen—or read—my lecture as it was given to those who really wanted to fulfill that long-ago dream that is still inciting them to make that change; fulfill their destiny of Writing that first novel. Ready? Are your climbing shoes on? Good! Here we go... time to climb the Writer's Craft Mountain!

My 13 Steps

There are 13 steps I usually follow when I Write and Publish my books. You may follow these simple steps or be inspired to create your own. There is a procedure you should follow when Writing and Publishing. Some of these writing methods and rules are written down somewhere, and it is best to follow them. When we drive our cars on the road, there are traffic lights we must obey. If we come to a stop sign or a red light, we know we have to look for obstructions and pedestrians in our way. We cannot override these issues, for they do exist. Such are our limitations. We cannot go beyond them, even if we really want to.

So what do we do? How do we begin to write? How do we know what to write? Where do we start? You may even say to yourself, "Oh God! Can I do this thing? Can I really write?"

We all must *Learn* to write. At one point, we had to do it in elementary school and in high school and our teachers made us write. Some of us wrote for our college classes. But that was required writing. Now, we want to write for our entertainment, our financial advancement, or maybe just because we want to express ourselves in written form or leave a legacy for our loved ones. How can we prove that we can write and write well? I like the "I CAN" part. I will continue to remind you that I have Dyslexia. If I can Write, so can you. Nothing is holding most of you back from writing but yourself.

My 13 steps are simple. I have to K.I.S.S my writing skills: <u>K</u>eep <u>I</u>t <u>S</u>imple <u>S</u>illy! Why not? It works for me. Will it work for you? I have no idea really; that is for you to determine. Why 13? Why not? You want more? Why want more? I say again, K.I.S.S your writing, unless you are writing professionally. If that is what you want to do, then this book is probably beneath you. Technical and Professional writers already grasp the concepts necessary for their craft. This book is for those who have a drive or passion within themselves for their Undiscovered Country, their passion for writing.

So let's venture into K.I.S.S. It is simple: writing is not as complex as you think. Then again, how much did you focus in school? Did you read in school? Do you read now? Do you read local newspapers or magazines? Do you read and comprehend well? How can you enhance your writing skills without reading? Isn't that like trying to cook a gourmet meal without ever having tasted good food? That is the real question.

STEP 1: READING AND WRITING YOUR STORY

If you don't Read or you don't like to Read, then just stop here. Here is the reality check of writing books:

- You have to Read!

- You have to know how to Read!

- You have to Read Words!

- You have to Read over a million words before you can even begin to Write!

- You have to Read or learn how to Read the DICTIONARY!

- You have to Read or learn how to Read a THESAURAS!

- You have to Read many books and Read other books and Read different kind of books, and then, keep on Reading!

Sorry for the reality check, but some wannabe writers do not realize the importance of reading.

Reading is a lot of work for some; and if you think it is, then writing is not for you. A college professor reads more than I do, as does a technical writer reads more than I do. A criminal lawyer and mechanical engineer read more than I do. Why? Because reading is part of what they do for a living. Writers pace themselves. We write when we feel like it. We write for fun. We write for a livelihood or self-satisfaction. We write out of habit or hobby. We write to tell stories trapped inside of our minds, as if a bird was trapped in a cage. These caged thoughts and ideas want their freedom too. Something inside of us can be bottled up like air in a soda can, and eventually, we have to burp. That burping is a release, and that release is your writing at its best.

Now back to Reading. Yes, I said Reading. I love it! I love those wonderful stories that took me away from my house, my job, my family, my relationships, my children... oops! I don't have any children, but you know what I'm talking about if you do.

When I was in school, I read *Betsy and Billy* by Carolyn Haywood, *The Long Black Coat* by Jay Bennett, *Hey God, It's Me, Margret* by Judy Blume, *Oliver Twist* by Charles Dickens, and Shakespeare's tragedies. Over a span of 35 years, I devoured every page of over 300 books, and that is only a minute fraction of all the other books I've read. Perhaps I am underestimating my library, but I have Read a lot: books, books, and more books!

The saddest part of my life was when my mother threw many of my books away during a spring cleaning episode. I came home from school and cried when I realized she'd cleaned out my library in my room and I had to start all over again, re-collecting the ones I lost as well as obtaining new ones.

I Read so many words growing up that it was difficult to even tell I was dyslexic. I knew I was, but it remained a secret for years. My sisters didn't know, and my mother was in denial. My elementary teachers knew and helped me immensely. The one thing I had to do to conquer my disability was to Read and study words. I memorized how the words should be spelled, and when my brain would joke with me, I stood firm like the one a mother who catches a child red handed with his hand in the cookie jar: I reprimanded my brain, "You do it right this time!" I was always a little hard on myself, but so are mothers who want their children to do the right thing. I gave my brain some tough love and told it with patience, "We will jump over these stumbling blocks, so don't quit now."

You can stroke your ego better than anybody else can. Only you can determine what you can and can't do and prove those wrong who try to discourage you. I could Read. I had to. I wanted to write my stories down, to unleash the thoughts within my mind's eye. I wanted to dream on paper. But before I did that, I wanted to read what other writers had to say. If they could put me on a train leading to a utopian community of words, ideas, thoughts, and imaginative worlds, I wanted a front seat.

My passion for reading is as great as my passion for writing. There is no difference. If you like to read, then Read. If you want to write, then Write. After you have read as much as I have, then you will find the one writer to model after. Who are your mentors? What writers take you flying above your house into the next town, the previous era, to the unspeakable world of conflict, the fantastic cloud that only exists in your mind's eye? What author makes you dream of the guy you wish you were in love with or could romance your soul?

I like young adult and general fiction, so that is what I usually focus on. Hey, that's just me. But what about you? What stories make you happy or touch you in some way? What do you like to daydream about? What stories make you want to write similar ones? Some people like romance novels. So do I, but that is not my true passion. I can't write good self-help books; I'm no Joel Osteen. There is only one of him, thank God! He is good at his craft of Writing and Speaking, and I like to read his books, because they are well written and very inspirational as well. Hey, if the book is good, why not read it? But just because I like Mr. Osteen's books does not mean I can or want to write the same kind. I've read all sorts of books and love them all. One of my favorite prose and poem books is *A Tear and a Smile* by Khalil Gibran, a Middle Eastern man who writes very well, and is worthy of my reading time.

Of course there are books I really detest. One genre I simply cannot venture into is urban fiction. I do not enjoy reading about a young kid whose parents are on drugs, a husband beating his wife, kids shooting kids, murder and prostitution among the young, child pornography, drug-infested streets, and so on. These not on my cool book list, but the truth is, they may be on yours.

I won't apologize for not liking urban fiction though. I'm not sorry, and I like what I like. You should feel the same. Your readers will like what you write, especially if it is written well. So stick what you like. A Writer's Craft may derive from many different gardens, different avenues, or different climates. Some writer's develop their craft among the jungles of Africa, some in the streets of London, England, some in the sexual atriums of Greece, some on Planet X or a newly named fantasy world, some in the most violent environments, and of course some—like mine—are from simple rose gardens. My book, *The Passing of Mother Mary*, is an inspirational story, telling how a child's destiny was placed in the hands of another. I was very emotionally moved as I wrote some of the chapters, so I knew my readers were going to be emotionally touched as well.

Many writers write better with each new manuscript. Some writers are always learning and improving their craft. Those writers who have a spiritual insight try to capture their reader's soul on paper, just like authors that fantasize about mystical things and imaginative places. God blesses all writers, as well as all readers. We are all in a world that stands alone. We do not sing, dance, or act. We Read and Write, which may seem boring to some, but for us, we are highly entertained and motivated as we engross ourselves in our Writer's Craft.

So now, do you still want to write? Then do like the little children. Sit Up and take notice of words. Stand Up and learn how to Read well. Read many genres, even those you are not familiar with or are not sure you will like. Walk over to the table or bookshelves that contain books. Run to the couch or chair or even your own bed and just Write! Jump at the chance to dream from the experiences someone else has implanted in through their books. Finally, make no make more excuses why you can't Read or Write You say you don't know how to write? Then what is stopping you from learning?

If a Dyslexic like me doesn't make excuses, why would you? Put your mind to it and just do it! I make no excuses for myself. I realized my limitations and then found a way to beat them. I Read books. I trained my brain to read and read well. I wanted to read another point of view of how the world was through someone else's eyes. I tried and cried and tried and tried again until I did it!

If you've managed to read this far, then let's go to Step 2.

Journal:

What Books Have Made You Want to Write?

(Think about the books you've read throughout your lifetime or the ones you are reading now. Which of them inspired you to write your own stories, thoughts, or ideas? Write them down here. I have given you a few examples.

1.   *A Tear and a Smile* by Kahlil Gibran

2.   *Family* by J. California Cooper

3.   *The Long Black Coat* by Jay Bennett

4.

5.

6.

7.

8.

9.

10.

A Good Tale

So, what do you like to write about? What stories can you come up with? How do your ideas emerge? What is your inspiration? Can you just write a short story, poem, or a prose from scratch, without any inspiration or thought put into it? If you are a creative being as I am, then you already know you have the intuition to develop your Writer's Craft. You have read the stories of others and have said to yourself, "If they can do it, so can I." You also have that dream particle already sparkling in your brain. Now get your pen or pencil and paper (or your laptop, if you prefer) ready. Put that dictionary and thesaurus right in front of you; you are going to need them. If you're using a computer, load up Microsoft Word. Now Brainstorm!

What's "brainstorming"? Brainstorming is just jotting your ideas down in no particular order or sequence. You must learn to rapidly brainstorm the ideas of your story; scenes, characters, storyline, timelines, plot, conflict, and situations. These ideas should be quickly jotted down on paper or typed, without hesitation, correction, or fine-tuning on the details.

Next, start the mapping or storyboard process of your book. One approach is to map out the story like a movie. Become the director of your own film. Most directors usually follow a storyboard, and you must learn to do the same when writing fictional novels. What happened first? Second? Third? Is there a flashback or a back-story? If you have a back-story, I suggest you tell that first. Some writers include the flashback in the middle or at the end of the book, but that can leave readers feeling lost and confused and asking, "Okay, wait... what happened again?" If a reader keeps flipping through the pages to find character names, locations, or prompts (objects that add intrigue to a storyline), the reader is not a detailed reader or the book has story flaws. In my book, *The Passing of Mother Mary*, my flashback is introduced first. The prompts are throughout the book, so yes, it requires a detailed reader.

Mapping out your story is not as easy as it sounds but it can be done. When you have completed a final draft of your story, you have not only mapped out the whole story for yourself, but also for your readers. The story should have a nice scene sequence or flow. I will illustrate more of the mapping process later.

Back to brainstorming, it is like dreaming with your eyes open. Are you dreaming of the story you wanted to write? How does the dream begin? How does it end? What happens in the middle of the dream? In brainstorming, your story is not finalized; it's only a draft. You are actually just throwing ideas on the paper. It becomes like a puzzle. You are settling the pieces on a table right out of the box in no particular order so you can begin positioning them in place, unscrambling them, and slowing snapping the sequences of the story in the order that you want it to be. Writers follow the yellow brick road of story writing, and then they move on!

STEP 2: WRITING YOUR STORY

Many people need some form of inspiration to write. Some need to be told what to write since they don't know themselves. Novice writers will not write until they have a mental urge to do so. There are lazy writers who will wait and try to pace themselves, thus wasting valuable time and creative energy. Don't be like this. Look inside yourself, and it will come. Don't think about it... just write!

Do you daydream? Where do your dreams take you? What do you dream about? I use to daydream a lot when I was young, so much so that the daydreams overwhelmed me and took away my playtime. I would sit for hours and cast my mind beyond my neighborhood. I went to California with all sorts of characters. I rebuilt invisible lives and made my characters travel to the ends of Earth and back again. Most of your dreams will spin from the mind's eye, the part of the brain that sees what the dreamer sees with bursts of energy and detailed imagery.

I took my daydreams from my mind's eye and wrote short stories. In my books, my characters are so real that you can envision their emotional turmoil, chaos, and periods of supreme joy. They may even be on an adventure. The writer has to be the first person to see their story being told as if it was through the eyes of the reader from start to finish. You have to know what the characters look like, what happens to them all the way to the end, where they are, and how they have gotten from place to place. You are the one who tells the reader what happens in the story and what has led up to that happening. You put the dream in someone else's head; flash the images in front of the reader's eyes. They must see this dream of yours come alive. Don't just tell the story without being visual. The blind person may not see, yet they know what fierce wind sounds like, what heat feels like, what sugar tastes like, and how rough the pavement is compared to the touch of grass. Don't underestimate your readers' ability to see the creativity of your craft because it's only written in words. They have an imagination too!

The readers read only what you have in store for your characters, and yes, they are interested in what happens to them. The hard part is how to keep your readers with you. If the story is good, you don't have to worry about the readers' interest. There are, of course, readers of all kinds. I like to write for young adult and general fiction readers. I love involving teenagers in my stories, although I don't care to involve them in situations they cannot get out of. As I write their storyline, I help them get out of turmoil and chaos. I put inspiration in their lives. How you depict your characters will be the life or death of your book; therefore, you must continuously awe your readers, thus convincing them to turn the page and keep reading.

I recently Read *Widow of the South* by Robert Hicks, *Family* by J. California Cooper, and *Kindred* by Octavia Butler. These stories kept me in awe. I wanted to read more and more chapters each night, even though I usually limit myself to a chapter or two—sometimes three a night—and then I Stop! I like to absorb the action in my mind gradually. If I finish a book in one night, then I can't dream about the next chapter's events. But that's just me. I like to soak up the chapters like a sponge. I review and replay certain scenes and particular dialogues in my head until I am thoroughly ready to devour the next couple of chapters.

A good story is like a good pizza, delicious and so full of flavor that you want that same pizza repeatedly. Some stories are so overwhelming that you desire to keep reading that particular genre. I don't read many romance stories, science fiction, or thrillers. Those stories have a certain audience, and the authors who write in those genres know that they need to tell a story to keep their audience wanting more.

Nora Roberts, for example, is a fantastic romance novelist, and she has a marketable audience.

I want my readers to see a unique character resolve their dilemmas with the help of another. I like to see my main characters rescued by strong sub-character(s). There has to be an infamous hero watching over my characters, like a mama bird watching over her young. I try to visualize each scene and sketch with vivid descriptions, like a Picasso artist. I try to write serious, yet sometimes humorous dialogue—sometimes-emotional dialogue that sends a tear down my cheek. Emotion is a very important asset to a good writer.

Am I perfect in my Writer's Craft? No! But I consider that leaving room for improvement. Did you ever go into a restaurant and eat so much that you didn't leave room for dessert? I always leave room for desert! I want to learn a lesson each time I write, and I like growth. All writers should make room for growth. Life is so full of experiences, and those experiences make for good stories and perhaps a good book. Don't ever think you should be a writer with a full plate. Scoot the veggies over, for your readers are waiting for your next creation.

Novice writers need to find mentoring authors who will save them time and not spin them into confusion when they are trying to decide what genre to follow. My mentoring Authors are Charles Dickens, the Bronte sisters, Harriet Beecher-Stowe, Robert Hicks, Charles Johnson, Khalil Gibran, Margret Walker, Octavia Butler, J. California Cooper, and a few others. Whose books do you read and enjoy or resonate with? What genre are they? I truly believe most authors have read the work of other authors within their genre prior to writing their craft. They have a huge knowledge base in their repertoire of stories. I have Read various books in order to visualize authors' ideas as if they are forming their ideas in front of me. My favorite Authors taught me how to Write, and I have learned some of their techniques. You must strive for this as well. Follow by example at first and then find your own way to express yourself.

To finalize this step, map out your story. Storyboarding is not as easy as you think, but you can handle it if you want to write. Mapping is different from brainstorming. You've already got the idea for your story, and you are no longer jotting down more ideas. Now, you are mapping. Write down your Characters and their names first. Common names can be a bore to some readers. Be creative. I know some writers that have gotten unusual names from the names of streets in their local city. Other writers have chosen names of famous people in history to represent their characters. Biblical names should be used with caution. For instance, Jesus is a Hispanic name as well as a biblical name, yet I would refrain from using it because on a worldwide scale, it will be associated with Jesus Christ, even if this is not your intention.

J. California Cooper chose names like Always, Soon, Plum, and Doak for her book, *Family*. I loved the story and its characters.

Octavia Butler used the name Rufe in her book *Kindred*. Iola was a character name in *Iola Leroy* by Frances E.W. Harper. In my book, *The Passing of Mother Mary*, I used my pen name, Brownlow. Your unique characters and their names should help the reader connect with your story even for a brief moment. Make the character names memorable so that the readers will recall who they are and what they have gone through, like Jane Eyre, Oliver Twist, Uncle Tom, Sicly, Lula, Vvry, John Coffe, and so on.

Now, for the Setting. Where are your characters? Are they in a city or town, on a boat, in a house, or traveling somewhere? What year is it? If you create a fictitious time or place for your setting, make it believable. This is one area where I feel I made my mistake in *The Passing of Mother Mary*. The cities in my book are not as descriptive as I wanted them to be. Fortunately, it did not really harm my storyline, but I got lucky on that. Once you have published your work, it is what it is—meaning, no more editing. So be sure to get it right the first time around.

Be as accurate as you can possibly be. If you are using a real time and place, do your research. For instance, characters wouldn't have cell phones until the mid-1980s, so if you are writing a book about the Roaring Twenties, the Dirty Thirties, or the Swinging Sixties, make sure they are not checking their voicemail!

Life is nothing without a little conflict. What is actually happening to the character? Action must be the first priority when writing a storyline. Are they in trouble, on an adventure, dying, being born in a certain era, or are they having issues with people, situations, or themselves? How do they resolve their conflicts? Would the reader agree with how the character fairs in the end? If the reader were in a similar situation, would the outcome be the same? Does the character's conflict hold the reader's attention enough for them to finish your book? This is a very important aspect. There must be a flow; a sequence of events that keeps the reader turning to the next page.

Thus, to my novice writers, I need to remind you that mapping out your storyline guides the flow of the story. The pieces of the puzzle (your story) are now arranged and can be assembled.

But now that you have the story mapped out, how do you begin to Describe your scenes? Let's find out!

Journal:

MAPPING: First Draft

(This is an example of mapping for *The Passing of Mother Mary*. Use this sample to do your own mapping!)

1. **CHARACTERS:** Brownlow, Mother Mary, Father Lauden, Phillip Talley...

2. **PLACE:** New Mexico. Iowa. Church. Palemos' house/Indian reservation

3. **TIME:** 1990s, 2000s-present day

4. **CONFLICT-** Can Investigator Phillip Talley find Brownlow in time after she escapes the wrath of Mother Mary Catherine?

5.

6.

8.

9.

Journal:

MAPPING: First Draft

1. Tiras rapes Myra.

2. Myra gives birth to Genueve and Mary Catherine and dies while in a coma.

3. Genueve gives birth to Brownlow and dies.

4. Brownlow is raised by Mary Catherine.

5. Mary Catherine mistreats Brownlow.

6. Father Lauden steps in to help Brownlow escape her aunt's rage.

7. Brownlow finally runs away with Mary Catherine chasing after her... (and the mapping continues).

8.

9.

My New World

Are you creating a new world? How good is your imagination? Do you know the area you are creating? Sometimes writers Create their own worlds. These writers take the time to draw their book's entire setting on paper. J. K. Rowling created the entire world of Hogwart's in her book series for *Harry Potter*. Where is Hogwart's? Is it a real place? Of course not, but she created it in her mind and then placed it on paper. A great imagination is just that—GREAT! How about J.R.R. Tolkien, the writer of *Lord of the Rings*? He takes us to the Shire with such description that we are enthralled to continue to read of that place and all that it entails.

STEP 3: DESCRIBING YOUR SCENCES

In your story, what is the world like? What point of view are you using? In my stories, I use both real and created locations. The American

States may be real, but I like creating the cities myself. I usually use cities close to the real ones. By creating new places, I use my mind's eye more. I want my readers to see new and exciting places. If I use a real place, I strive to be accurate in how I present that place or era. Some readers are more knowledgeable about locations than writers may realize. Accuracy is very important to many readers. There are a lot of readers who deliberately look for inconsistencies in a writer's work. Are you making your location a real place? Then map the place as accurately as you possibly can. If the place is not real, then make it convincing. Let your readers see what you, the writer, sees. I see and focus on my imaginary locations as I am writing about them. I can't afford to leave out details, for they are far too important. If you can't keep the details in your mind straight, then map them out on paper.

The timeline is just as important as the location. In the book *Widow of the South* by Robert Hicks, the writer sets up the timeline in the opening pages. The first character you encounter as a reader may not be the main character, but that person should tell you when and where we are. In this book, right away, I knew it was the Civil War Era, and I was instantly hooked because I enjoy Civil War novels.

The description of the Character within the first two pages helps as well. How are people dressed? What is their speech pattern? Do they have a Northern accent? A Southern drawl? Do they use East Coast or West Coast slang? Do they speak North American or European English?

If there are prompts (objects) that are discussed, be sure those objects would have existed in that era. We've already mentioned cell phones as one example, but you don't want a machine gun in the Civil War era unless you are writing something having to do with time travel or science fiction or something like Harry Turtledove's *Guns of the South,* which is an excellent book.

I will say it again: make the world in your book as real and as believable as you can. Consider your audiences as you write. Writing without thinking about readers' rejection is not good writing. Your world should not be written in retaliation to what has happened to you in your real world, for this will be too transparent and will turn your readers away. Why sabotage your Writing Craft? For instance, there are a lot of angry women who have been hurt by their companions, husbands, friends, and associates, but why launch your fury with your readers? They weren't a part of your tragedy. Your experiences in life will be something you draw on as you write, but you should never use your book as a means to vengeance, because your readers will be caught in the crossfire and will not enjoy your book.

My books, as with all my writings, are purely from the inner part of me. I want my readers to be a part of my world as I've created it. I want them to see what I see, hear what I hear, feel what I feel, taste what I taste, and touch what I touch. Put all your senses in your description of your world. Make your created world as real as possible!

The characters in your created world must be believable as well. The characters must illustrate that they are a member of that created society. For instance, Captain Spock is a Vulcan. He is not from Planet Earth, yet he fits in in a most believable way as an important crewmember of the *Starship Enterprise* on *Star Trek*. SpongeBob SquarePants lives in the sea in a place called Bikini Bottom, as do most of the other characters on that show. They all fit there, whether it is a starfish or a squirrel in a waterproof helmet. The characters must use accurate, time-sensitive means of communication. Bugs Bunny world did not have a cell phone or Blackberry, but he did occasionally mail letters. Your readers aren't stupid, and they won't appreciate being made a fool of, so remember that they know one time frame or era from another.

Your characters must also fit the genre. I would never put the widow from *Widow of the South* in my book, *The Passing of Mother Mary* because a character like that would have no reason to be there. The dialogue used in my book is too modern, and there are accents that would not correlate with the widow's Civil War-era accent. Keep your characters in perspective so you can keep your readers' attention.

Description is the third and most important entity of the Writer's Craft. As a writer, I have to remember that all my readers are totally blind and deaf; I have to tell my readers what they are seeing and hearing. They have no idea where they are until I describe the surroundings to them. How acute is a reader's sense of hearing? Well, they are as mute as the paper they're reading! If you want them to Hear what you are saying, you have to do literary sign language for them. This means you have to totally describe what the character Hears and does. The reader will never guess your intentions, nor should you want them to. The reader is new to your book therefore; give them a little insight on what is going on. Do you Hear me?

If the characters in my story Smell something, what is it? Is it a smell sweet, or horrid like a burning tire? When my character Touches something, is it smooth and silky, rough and coarse, slick or slimy, hot or cold? What my character feels, the reader should share the same senses. What is your character Eating or Drinking? Should the reader know what your character Tastes already? Tell the reader what is for breakfast, lunch, or dinner. If there are snacks, make the reader's mouth water with your description of them.

All your Descriptions in your writing should make the reader feel at ease with what you've written, not as if they are being duped or tricked into believing something unbelievable. Descriptions make your story intensely visible to the reader who is technically blind, mute, and unable to feel or smell what your character feels and smells until you tell them.

Remember: Above all, you as the writer must create the senses of your characters. The reader will be curious about these senses. Without describing your world in detail your book will be dry, unbelievable, and a chore for your readers to get through. Your characters only exist in the mind of the reader, and so they should be as human as your reader. As a Writer, you don't merely exist; you are a participant in your Character's life—in fact, the sovereign god and controlling power of their world. Shouldn't your reader be a participant of your character's environment as well? The Bible describes how the Earth was built in seven days. As writers, we need to create our worlds and everything in it for our readers. We need to describe what the reader needs to see, hear, feel, touch, and taste.

The Writer is always the first Reader I could never be part of the world in my own books if I hadn't read them thoroughly. I took my time and focused. I mapped certain scenes, locations, people, objects, landscape, and so on. You must do the same.

It's your story. It's your world, real or imaginative. Give your readers something believable to focus on. Describe Everything!

Journal

DESCRIPTION: Draft

(Describe your entire home using all your senses.)

1. **SIGHT**: Big house, white and blue, 1,100 sq. feet

2. **HEARING**: Quiet and serene.

3. **SMELL**: Rose-smelling candles and potpourri

4. **TOUCH**: Plush, soft, comfortable furniture with foreign embroidery

5. **TASTE**: Warm chocolate chip cookies from the plate in the kitchen

The Skills of the Craft

So you've got an Idea. You have Mapped out your story, and you've got the Descriptions in your head. What skills do you need to proceed? How talented are you? Yes, it does take talent to broaden the horizons of your reader's mind. Do you like fiction? Nonfiction? Self-help books? Textbooks? Religious books?

I prefer fiction. Fiction for young adults captured my attention first in *The Long Black Coat* by Jay Bennett. Jay has a talent for telling a good tale in a way a young adult would understand. The first skill is to know your audience. Who are they? Young, mature, middle-aged, older groups, or the elderly who can still read with or without glasses?

The first skill for me was to decide who I wanted to write for. My nephew helped me decide that. He was a teenager, and I wanted to write a story he could read and enjoy. I had to make it an adventure story with twists and turns.

I knew my limitations, and so must you. I am no J. K. Rowling! Science fiction is not my genre. Self-help books, like this one you're reading, are written by those who know what they're talking about or have some experience you haven't had, and they want to share. "the fruits of the vine," as my grandmother would often say, or pass the hat of wisdom to the next generation. I know what I know, and so I share the knowledge. Write about what you are familiar with. Write using the talents within you that interest you most. If you Write beyond your limitations, you may lose your readers and even become bored with your own writing. Can you keep your Craft within you vision? Can you create something great? How do you develop your Craft?

STEP 4: CRAFTING

I Craft my stories from my very own head. Many people can't do that. Some people have to write their ideas down on paper. In our computer age, we use computers that are supplied with Microsoft Word or Note Pad. Some software programs help the writer by walking them through the writing process.

This is where the local workshops come in. Reeducating yourself in the Writing Process is not a bad idea. You have to start somewhere, right? There are so many books to Read that will help you get to where you need to be as a Writer. It will take time to read the ones you may needed for your Craft.

I read *On Writing* by Stephen King, and it was so informative, that I still Read it over and over again. You have to do some research and educate yourself. Refusing to read a book that you know will be informative and help you in the long run is pure laziness. Don't do that to yourself! If you are a churchgoer, you know that you've read the same Bible stories over and over again throughout your lifetime. If Reading the Bible repetitiously is supposed to help you embrace your spiritual faith, then why not Read a book about writing, about perfecting your Craft?

I highly suggest you Read *Writing a Novel* by John Braine. He has illustrated his Craft patiently in words and expressed how to reinforce the Writer's Craft, which has helped me to develop mine.

I want those who want to Write to Write with confidence despite any limitations they may have. Believe me,, it is not easy to live with Dyslexia, but I Write stories, tales, poems, and prose. As I've told you, I have learned by Reading stories of others, daydreaming and putting stories in my own head, Crafting, learning the writing process, and doing what I love to do... Write!

College writing courses can definitely help writers, but it is not always a financially viable option. Either you know your Craft or you don't, and reeducating yourself for the sake of your Craft may be worth your time and money. Many novice Writers just give up when they find out that they have to have additional writing skills in order to creatively Craft stories, poems, or prose. There is no time to be lazy or procrastinate. You must find a way to perfect your Craft If you can, attend some writing workshops and conferences. In addition to educating you, this will also give you the opportunity to network with those just like you... the Writer.

As stated earlier, I took many composition writing courses, creative writing courses, poetry classes, and literature classes. I had to relearn how to Write and Write well. I had to tap into my mind's eye that was the nucleus of my Craft.

My writing classes and the books I've Read have taught me different styles of Writing. I had to learn the different genres in order to know which one I wanted to write in.

One way to develop your Craft is to familiarize yourself with those most famous Crafters who ever lived. Let them mentor you with their Crafting of words, phrases, sentencing, composing, description, and imagination. Yes, you have to Read their stories in order to develop yours in a similar fashion. I had to Read stories from the classic crafters: the dialogues of Plato, the testaments of the Bible, Grimm's fairytales, Shakespeare's tragedies, masterpieces by Charles Dickens and Harriet Beecher-Stowe, and so many others that widened my eyes to the Craft of writing.

Remember that dream you had a few days ago? How about just jotting it down? What was it about? How did it begin? What happened in the middle? How did it end? Some stories are just that: dreams. Many authors have just dreamed and dreamed big. They saw their dream in the mind's eye, that focal point of creating thoughts and ideas, and something twitched in the frontal lobe of their brains that told them to Write it down. I rarely jot my dreams down on paper. They stay in a lockbox within the deepest crevice of my brain and erupt like volcano, pushing those ideas to the surface when I need them. But that's me... and a little bit of Mozart, I suppose.

So if you have the desire to really Write the story you've dreamed about, then you must dedicate yourself to knowing your Craft and developing it through writing courses, mentors, and Reading the stories of the classic crafters.

Crafting is hard for those who don't Read. If you have Read classic novels or poems or seen classic movies or plays, then you can visualize the Writer's Craft from those Writers, Authors, Playwrights, and Orators. Don't imitate them or copy their works, for that's plagiarism, which is nothing more than cheating! Instead, learn from them and develop your own Craft. You've got talent or what it takes to write if you are reading this book. You have a Craft inside of you that just has to be fished out of a vast sea of confusion by a good fisherman. If you have read *The Old Man and the Sea* by Ernest Hemingway, you know about the fisherman's instinct and perseverance, two required qualities for writers.

Another skill you need for your Craft is to be able to put common reference books to good use, namely the dictionary and the thesaurus.

These contain a vast array of words that you really need to know and learn. Learn how to use the dictionary well and it will become your new best friend. With this great tool, you will at least be able to spell correctly. As Dyslexia I keep my dictionary always close at hand when I write. Next to the dictionary, I turn to my thesaurus. Words have to be chosen, weighed, sorted, arranged, committed, utilized, accessed, recovered, obtained, retrieved, and recaptured. You get the point, and Webster and Roget will help you do it.

Without a pen or pencil, a notebook or pad, a computer, or a flash drive, you will not be as efficient as you can be when you begin the Writing Crafting. Without a dictionary or, thesaurus, you have no craft. New, exciting words will make our story come alive outside of ourselves.

So there you are. You may need some writing classes or workshops, and you will need to Read other books illustrating the Writer's Craft. You will also need stationery, a computer, a flash drive, a dictionary, and a thesaurus. Above all, you need the instinct to unlock your talents within your mind's eye—to find that imaginative particle to get you started. Do you have these things and that talent? If you do, let's move on to your storyline.

Journal:

Skills and Tools for Your Craft

(List the skills and tools that will help your craft.)

1. Dictionary

2. Thesaurus

3. Pen, paper, computer, flash drive

4. Notes from brainstorming and mapping

5. Elements of Style by E. B. White

6. *On Writing* by Stephen King

7. *On Writing* by Stephen King

8. *Writing a Novel* by John Blaine

9. *Publish Basics* by Johnson/Pramschufer

10. *Write to Learn* by Donald M. Murray

Drama Begets Drama

Many people tell me they want to Write a book, and when they do, I ask, "What kind of book, and what is it about? Will it be fiction or nonfiction?" Many say they have no idea what their book will be about—that they just want to Write one. I simply shake my head in disappointment.

Those who really want to Write a book have their roots already grounded like a tree. In fact, they know they want to Write something long before they actually commit themselves to the task. I knew I wanted to Write short stories and prose. I also instinctively knew I wanted to Write a fiction novel. If you really want to Write a book, you will make every attempt to do so. You will not waste one more minute of your time, for you know there is no time to waste. If you are a writer, then you will Write! Go ahead and get the necessary skills together and take that famous Writer's leap. As I Write fiction, I daydream constantly about how my story is supposed to flow. I dream about who will be the protagonist and who will be the antagonist. I also dream about what might possibly happen in each chapter. Yes, I dream about my Craft, and you should too.

By the way, that dream is your casting call. Your nose is twitching, and your ears are ringing. Your soul has a little person on your shoulder saying, "Do it now! Write your story!" Don't listen to the evil twin on the other shoulder telling you there's no use for you to write, that you are no good, and that nobody will like your stuff. I heard that little devil say that stuff to me, and for a while, I put my work in a trunk somewhere in my house. When I heard the good twin in my mind, stalking me, continuously asking, "When are you going to finish your manuscript?" I shook my head and sighed deeply. That good twin entered my dreams, woke me up, and harassed me until finally, after six months, I angrily went to the trunk, grabbed my work, and finished manuscript. All I could say was "Thank God for the good twin."

I love dramatic stories. *The Color Purple* by Alice Walker is a dramatic novel as well as a movie. I went through a lot of emotions while I Read the book, but when the movie came out, those emotions really attacked my inner soul. That's what good Writing is all about. If Writers can capture the souls of their readers and make them happy, sad, angry, weeping, or even bewildered by the story's end, then that's a Writer!

When I wrote the scene for *The Passing of Mother Mary* about the character Brownlow ripping the only dress she had and crying to the angels to alleviate her pain, I cried! I was the Writer and the first Reader! A dramatic scene is just that: dramatic. If the character John Coffe in Stephen King's *The Green Mile* didn't reveal the emotional flashbacks, describing another character's previous events, which also put him on the green mile with John Coffe, I would have thrown the book in the trash. Even Stephen King knew his readers had to feel John Coffe's emotional turmoil as revealed in that story. We needed to know why the dramatic remembrances were so sensitive to the main character. Not revealing the dramatic scene teases and irritates the reader, and they will likely tell others that the book is lame, empty, or wooden because the Writer carelessly left something important out.

When Writing a dramatic novel, you have to trap your reader as if they are in a bear trap and send a wolf slowly stalking toward them, ready to devour them. The fear alone is dramatic. Just when that wolf is about to pounce on them, there must be an unforeseen shot that rings out and strikes the wolf, maiming him. That which releases the reader is called a dramatic release. You have to release the reader from the drama. Keeping the reader prisoner in a dramatic part of your book not only angers the reader, but also tires them out before they can get to the end of the story. Don't do that! Keeping your readers at bay is okay for a brief moment, but you must release them if you want them to come back to your library of stories. They will come back if you alleviate the Character's distress, thus calming your reader's emotional distress at the same time.

STEP 5: THE STORYLINE

My nephew called my cell phone and told me he had a story he wanted to write. I asked him what the storyline was, and he could not tell me. He just said it was about vampires. That got my attention, so I told him to follow my lead and Write his story according to how I Write mine and then modify it as he learned the basics.

Just like my nephew, you, my fellow reader, can also follow my lead. Let's start by reviewing one of my short stories, and we will rewrite a similar short story together. A novice Writer should start with a short story first. Writers must show growth, so it is okay to Write a teaser for your readers, and that's a short story.

Ready?

The title of my story is, 'My Grandma Dreams." Now, write your title. You don't have one? Then don't worry about it now; it will develop on its own in time. If you worry about the title now, you will forget your purpose, which is to focus on the story itself. Worry about the title later.

One of my stories involves an old woman going through the middle stages of Alzheimer's. She constantly dreams of the past. Bria, her granddaughter, coaxes her grandmother into telling her how her twin siblings were kidnapped. They were four at the time. As Bria and her grandmother return to their native city of Carver, Illinois, Bria helps solve the sixty-year-old missing person's case.

I like the storyline. It pleases me, and it's supposed to. If it doesn't please your audience, will you stop writing altogether or will you write just for your audience? For God's sake, don't waste your time on pleasing your audience! You have to Write for yourself first. If the storyline is good, your audience will enjoy it too. Be Creative. Think of a story that is unique and unusual, one that puts a character in a situation that is not the norm. Make it your story. Don't take someone else's idea just because you don't have one. You are a Writer, and your ideas will come if you just let them inside your mind's eye willingly.

Take your time, and your story will come to you naturally. It should if you are a Writer. You already have the Writer's Craft if you are reading this book. You have ideas; just them flow and don't try to force them out. Dream of your story and let your imagination rain down in droves. Write out what as many ideas as you can to describe what you want your story to be about. Be artistic like Picasso or Michelangelo. Writing is also considered an art form, a Craft, so from here on out, you will be considered an artist There is no time in your life to doubt yourself or your abilities. That's why you're reading this book, remember?

In the short story I'm Writing, the main Characters are Bria and her grandmother. Who are your main characters? My Setting is in Davenport, Kentucky and Carver, Illinois. Where do you place your Characters? How are you Describing your Setting? Use as much detail as you can.

Start your story with a bang! Write something unexpected. You have to hook the reader into your story, and the best place to do that is in the first few pages. You have to keep the reader's interest, so have the awe effect ready. If your characters and locations are fictional, then make them believable. Make your characters feel and act like you or people you know. Make the storyline interesting and different.

Don't over-criticize your characters or put them in a situation in which you will receive adverse opinions from your readers. If you attack your audience, you will also lose them at the same time. As we've discussed, the Writer's Craft should not be written in retaliation of your actual living situation. Don't make your writing too personal, and don't try to use it to get revenge. It's not your readers' fault that you are where you are or that you are in the situation you're in. Just Write a good story. Write for yourself first, and your readers will like it if it is worthy of their time.

Use your own speech pattern or tone or even create one. If it is a foreign tone, make sure your reader will pick that up. Use a particular tone, dialect, or common usage of words to give the reader an indication as to where you are and what timeline you are focusing on.

The Climax or Plot of your story will enter the story without you really focusing on it. The Writer's Craft is placed on the storyline. Most creative Writers have the natural ability to tell a story without a lot of effort. If you have something to say, your Writer's Craft will say it for you. Don't get frustrated about that which comes naturally to a Writer.

The ending should be like the beginning: purely unexpected. If the ending is emotional, make sure it is a positive emotion. You want your readers to be happy with you. Don't take your readers to a funeral without some positive reinforcement. If you, the Writer, are thrilled about the storyline, so will your readers be. Just don't lose focus.

Have fun Writing a good storyline. Remember the Writer's Craft is just that: the ability to Craft a good tale, first for yourself and then for your readers. Have fun putting your characters in a situation that you may not find yourself in. Have fun surprising your readers by going somewhere unexpected. Have fun developing your storyline. Just have fun, Writers! The Writer's Craft is and will always be fun and entertaining. Now Write a sample story and have fun doing it!

MY GRANDMA DREAMS

(An Excerpt of First Draft)

"My grandma dreams. As she dreams, she talks. Grandma Paul talks in her sleep. I thought it was okay at first, that her stories and tales were unique. I hated to hear some of them, though, but I had no choice. My mother forced me to take care of Grandma Paul. I didn't think Grandma Paul was that old. She was in her late sixties. She could do a lot of things herself, but not always. She did need someone to help with her dressing and fixing food at times. No one else wanted to do it, so I had to. Although I was afraid at first, I stayed with her in the house..." Bria halted her writing.

Grandma Paul was coming out of the kitchen. She laid the pancakes in the center of the table and set the bacon beside them. Grandma Paul smiled at Bria as she went back into the kitchen.

Bria returned to her notebook and wrote her last note. "...I was taking care of her every day and night. After hearing these stories, I suddenly became obsessed. I don't know why. It was what it was. My mother came by the house a few times, but I refused to talk with her. I was angry that she made me take care of Grandma Paul by all by myself. When my mother did visit, Grandma Paul made me stay in the same room while she was there. I never told her about Grandma Paul's dreams or her stories, but I do remember them as clearly as I remember when she whispered them..."

"Eat, child. Put that book away." Grandma returned to the table with her tea. She put a cube of sugar in it and stirred. After taking a sip, she proceeded to fix her plate of eggs, bacon, and pancakes. Grandma ate quietly.

The silence often killed me. I wanted to shout, but what good would that do? I ate alone and in silence.

After we finished breakfast, my tutor knocked on the door. Grandma looked at me. I knew the routine. I stood to get the door. He entered with a smile. I hated his smile; it was crooked and mocking. A tall man in a pressed suit, well groomed and very articulate, waited for me to smile back, but I didn't.

He walked in to the sitting room and said, "Well now, where's Mrs. Lipton?"

"In the kitchen, cleaning up."

"Well, let's get started, shall we?"

"Of course."

After my tutor left, I headed for my room. Grandma Paul was on the sofa, and yes, she was dreaming again. I halted my steps. I sat on the floor close to her. As I twiddled my thumbs, she began to dream.

"Matte, I'm tellin you the truth...they ain't here...they went with Mr. McGill...he took 'em in his car...I don't know where he took' em...we was just walkin' along...he told them to get in his car...he'll take 'em the rest of the way...sorry, Matte...I don't know what to do...'

"As I sat and listened, I tried to recall the story. As I remember Mama telling me, Matte was Grandma Paul's mother. I don't know why she always called her mother by her first name, but her other children had gone missing and were gone for a long time. They sent out a search party three times, but they still could not find those twins. Mr. McGill had disappeared too. He was a new resident in Carver, and he was a suspect in the kidnapping.

"Grandma Paul was only nine years old at the time. She had gone into the woods to feed some stray dog when the twins were taken. They were only five years old at the time. When she got back to the road, Mr. McGill just looked at her. Grandma Paul told my mama that he just didn't take her, and she doesn't know why..."

That was the first draft of one of my first short stories. I really like the ending; it was sad yet satisfying. You can read more of this story in my book, *The Tales from the Gardens.* Short stories like this one are sometimes the best stories to read to a child at bedtime or just waiting for your car to be fixed at the dealership. Writing such stories is a great pastime for any writer, and it will help you practice and hone your Craft.

The most important thing to a storyline is the dramatic ending. I like to end a story with an emotional or humorous event or twist. It's the Wow effect that makes the reader smile as they close the book and say, "Wow! That was a great story." In *Kindred* by Octavia Butler, I closed the book with a smile on my face and said, "Wow!"

You want your book to have a great storyline. You need one, and your readers will only pick up books that they feel will overwhelm them like a movie. So take your time configuring your storyline; no need to rush this part. The beginning of your story must be able to hook the reader like a great bass at the end of your fishing line; you reel them in with the middle part or the climax; and you finally release them as the story ends. With your talents in creativity and imagination, I know your storyline will be the trophy at the end of your Writing project.

Journal:

Ideas for a Short Story

(Got any great ideas for a short story? Sure you do! Write them here and then refer back to this page when you write that story!)

Drafting

By the end of Writing your first story, you have just completed the first draft. Hooray for You! Now, you must continue your journey. It's not the time to stop for any reason. Read and Edit your first draft yourself. Add all the details you left out while you were just trying to get the storyline down. Now the story is written and the forgotten details are put in. How does the story look to you now? Drafting is all about answering the questions that the reader may ask: Who? What? When? Where? And How? As a Writer you must be prepared to answer those questions. Filling in all the lost details is called revising. You must revise until there is nothing left but the storyline. The storyline needs a Title. The Title you choose gives your story substance. Congratulations, Writers You have finished what is called, a completed Manuscript!

When I Write a story, it comes directly from my head. I just type it. I already know what is happening in each chapter as if it was already written before. Some Writers cannot do this. If you are one of these people, then don't worry about it so much; it's really no big deal, and all writers are different.

Sometimes, I do have to map the story details down in a small black journal. In that journal are my notes on the Characters, Setting, Storyline, intricate Details, and the Prompts I need to remember. I always save my work on a disk or flash drive. I read the first copy of my manuscript at least six times before doing a total revision or saving the second draft. This is your next step. Don't get lazy now! You've come too far to turn back.

Thus, I say again: Step up Writers!

STEP 6: FIRST DRAFT/REVISING

Thus far, we have scribbled intricate notes about a storyline or Idea. We've mapped out the

Details of the storyline and its Characters. We've figured out our Setting, developed various Descriptions (including sensory details), created the Plot and Conflicts and finally put the story's beginning, middle, and end together. This is an example of a route you can take, but it doesn't always happen with every story. You should be ready to Write or have already Written your first draft.

So now what?

Read what you have written. Does it make sense? Does the story flow? Did you answer all the questions that need to be answered? Remember, you're not only going to be the Writer of this manuscript, but also its first Reader. Thus, you must determine how it sounds to you? If you don't like it, will your readers?

So now what?

Read it again, slowly this time, and try to visualize what you have written and revise the story to where it makes even more sense. How many times should you read the story? Less than six times means you are a lazy Writer, and that will come through in your story. Don't be lazy You wanted to Write a story, right? Then as my grandmother would say, "Do it right or not at all!"

If you are Dyslexic like me, try Reading what you have written first, but allow an experienced proofreader to be the next person to review your manuscript. I will say it again: I refuse to let any limitations stop me from Writing and a proofreader will always be my best evaluator.

Revising is not a bad thing. If you have to take out paragraphs or change a phrase or two, then just do that. Spelling, grammar, and punctuation mean a lot to a manuscript. Spelling must be accurate. For this reason, using a computer is helpful. With Microsoft Word and other common word processing software, some common typos and spelling errors are immediately corrected as you type. With a computer, you can Write your first draft of your story a lot faster and change the words on a page or in a paragraph more rapidly than if you had written it on paper. Thank God for the world of technology; computers and word processing software are a godsend for writers.

Saving your work should be a major priority always save the first daft on your computer or flash drive so you can compare it with your second draft. Then attempt to rewrite the revised portions of your manuscript. By saving the first draft and then completing the revision you can learn to Write and Write better each time.

You shouldn't need a proofreader to help with your first draft, but some writers can't live without proofreaders. In that case, I say, why should they? A second set of eyes can put a Writer at a major advantage.

Using family members to proofread is usually not a good idea, so I've learned. Most family members are biased. They don't want to upset you, so they will sugarcoat their critique and seldom tell you when there are obvious things that need to be changed or corrected so they don't hurt your feelings or insult you. I have been writing since the age of fourteen, and during the years, some family and friends have read some of my work. Some of them really liked it, but only a few have encouraged me to continue my Craft. Other family members still haven't Read any of my books at all. This is not because they have anything against me or what I might have to say, but because they don't Read books at all. Not all of your family members or friends will be a part of your fan club. Sorry, but that's the reality, folks! Thus, never focus on what they will want to Read and approve of. Write for you first!

Allow your first true reader of your story (besides yourself) to be someone outside your inner circle. Proofreaders who are not family, friends, or associates may be just what you need to give you an objective review. Be open to their suggestions. Always advise the proofreader that it is your first draft and that you are lenient and able to revise your work if necessary.

After everything is Read and corrected to your satisfaction, you can move on. You have done well thus far, and even I am proud of your efforts. I, a Dyslexic will not stop now, nor should you. You have a good manuscript—a wonderful story and now a fine book. So take a huge leap of faith and publish what you have written! Publish it for yourself first, family and friends second, and third make to some money. Congratulations for you are a Writer an artist! But as Han Solo warned Luke, "Don't get cocky yet. It ain't over yet, kid."

Before you climb any more steps, let's rest and do some deep breathing. Let's recap, remember what we've learned, and rethink all we have discussed.

Recap

Let's break down everything we've learned. To recap is to review. I use these steps when I write, so let's recap which are the most important for you to focus on:

1. **IDEAS.** Find out if you are a Writer by spending a few hours alone, perhaps while you are driving a long distance, sitting in the doctor's office, waiting in line at the bank, or even doing your Sunday chores. Try to daydream about a place you've always wanted to visit, a person you've always wanted to share a romance with, how you might change the life or situation of someone you know, or even about encouraging someone in a bad predicament. How about resolving an issue in your own way? If you can daydream about any of these things in detail, then you can Write about them, and in your own poetic way.

2. **READ.** Reading other authors' work helps Writers to daydream just as that author did before he/she wrote and published their stories. You'll find so much information about the Craft of another Writer as you Read their work. The imaginative places, people, worlds, situations, and drama surrounding a character's life can stimulate the Writer's Craft for you, the future Writer. By Reading other books, you can put yourself in one of the character's places. You can feel what the character feels, see what the character sees, and understand what happens to the character from start to finish. By Reading the works of others, you enhance your creativity, and you learn to Write and Write well.

3. **MAPPING/BRAINSTORMING.** When you are ready to Write your story, the first step is to brainstorm and map out your story with the preliminaries.

Mapping out the characters involved in your story. What do they look like from head to toe? What do they sound like or act like? Where are they from, and where will they end up in your story? What situations are they in from start to finish? Describe the setting and be vivid. map your story from the point of a narrator or the character. Chose the POV (point of view) wisely. Use the dialogue of the era within the story. Watch the usage of words that reflect the timeframe of your story. Finally watch the flashbacks and the prompts. Don't rely on mental notes about the objects or prompts used in your story (for example, a diary, gun, newspaper article, jewelry, etc.) Instead, use a notebook (the same one you use to brainstorm) to record the objects used to explain an occurrence or something to help the reader understand what's happening.

4. **STORYLINE.** It is your story that must be adored. You must Write for yourself first. If the story is good as you wrote it, your audience will be just as entertained. Use all your tools to enhance your Craft: a dictionary, a thesaurus, and your own way of wording phrases and telling a story. One of the greatest mistakes is to Write in anger or for vindication. Your readers are not the source of your pain. Therapeutic writing is good for you, but it may target an audience unnecessarily. Reserve your therapeutic writing safely in the pages of your private journals.

5. **WRITING.** Now just Write the story. Use your time wisely. The biggest mistake is to rush your story. The readers will catch your mistakes if you don't. Learn the vocabulary necessary to complete your story. You must consider your audience when you Write

If you are Writing for adults, use language adults can relate. If you are Writing for a child, then use age-appropriate language. If you're Writing fiction, remember to hook your readers from chapter to chapter. Don't leave any information out and don't leave the readers hanging in awe or confusion. Don't worry about the number of pages or the amount of words. Stick to the storyline and don't focus on the ending; the story will write itself if you allow it to. Take your time, because a good story must be seasoned and have time to grow and develop. Think of it like carrying a baby; the birth of a baby is never too late. Like that baby, your story will come out in its own marvelous timing.

6. **EDIT/REVISE.** Now that you have finished your story, you have to either it Edit yourself or find an editor. Using your family members is really a bad

idea. Family members may take their time reading your story when you have a timeframe in mind to have your project completed. Try using an English or journalism major from a local college or university. College students who are in their senior year can be contacted through the college English professors. These students don't know you and will remain unbiased when they Read your material. J.K. Rowling did the same with her book series, *Harry Potter*, she allowed students from a nearby school to Read her story, and it was their word-of-mouth that got her started. I am Dyslexic, so I have a few proofreaders on standby, and I am not ashamed to use them. If you can edit your story yourself, that's great, but there is nothing wrong with another set of eyes. As most Writer's know, errors that seem to creep into every story. I remember seeing one in *Uncle Tom's Cabin* by Harriet Beecher-Stowe, and it's a classic! The errors in that novel didn't destroy the storyline, now did it? Your goal should be to get your story 99 percent error-free.

7. **COMPLETED.** Once you have a finished manuscript with all the corrections, let a proofreader Read it. The proofreader should be one who Reads If you choose one of your family members or a friend, make sure they are avid readers. You want a proofreader that can give you a positive, unbiased review with constructive critique. Remember, you should be the first Reader. I have Read my books several times before publishing them, and I like the stories I wrote. I like the storylines, descriptions, and, of course, my characters. If I am impressed with my book, I know my readers will also be. My story is now complete, and I am pleased with the results. I can now

publish my story. I am a Writer and I Write If you are a Writer, then you will start a Writing project and see it through to its completion. You will be just as pleased as I was when mine was completed.

So if you are a Writer then Write and follow these steps thoroughly until your story is fully completed. If you have this dream of Writing inside of you, now you have to let it liberate your soul. Do it now, not later! You just climbed the first crucial steps of the Writer's Craft. Take another deep breath, because now you have to climb the following Publishing steps. You can do it just as I have done. Ready or not, we're moving forward.

PUBLISHING YOUR NOVEL

Before You Submit

Once you have finished Writing your precious chapters, revising, proofreading, and taking care of all the necessary editing, you might be ready to submit your work to a printer or a publishing house, or *are you?*

Once the manuscript of your story is ready to be Published, you are also ready to change your status. You will no longer be considered just a Writer but now you will be called a Published Author. Therefore, you know you have to protect your work. Not protecting your Craft is ludicrous All your work was not done in vain! This is what you have you have sweated many minutes, hours, days, weeks, months, and perhaps years over, right? You had an idea, a creation, a Craft, and now you want to gift-wrap it for your readers. If this is true, then for your sake, protect what you have written.

How do you do that? Follow the next step! Copyright It!

My work is important to me. All those ideas are my intellectual property, and they belong to me and me alone. The characters breathe through me, and I through them. The setting is my utopian society, no matter how serene or violent it may be. It is the world, society, existence in which I create in my mind's eye. It is my perfection, and no one else's. My story is like a unique child: vulnerable. I've had to hover over it and shield it from any type of peril. For all those reasons, I always patent my invention of words and Copyrighted it at the first available moment!

STEP 7: COPYRIGHT YOUR WORK

There are three basic ways to copyright your Craft.

1. After I finished my manuscript, I Mailed it to myself and put it in my fireproof file cabinet when it was delivered by the postmaster, unopened. If you open the envelope, you will break the postmarked seal which will protected your rights as the owner. Only the author of the manuscript knows what is inside, therefore if you maintain the seal, you maintain your ownership. So Mail yourself your own manuscript, let yourself sign for it, then put it in a safety deposit box at your bank or under lock and key in a fireproof safe in your own home. You won't regret it believe me. Sound silly? Not to an experienced judge in a court of law it won't!

2. I also sent my manuscript to the Library of Congress Copyrighting office. You can file your rights directly. You can request a form from the Library of Congress. This form assures you that

your work is registered and cannot be plagiarized Be aware there is some cost involved, and it can take up to six months to get a certificate of registration But once you received the certificate of registration you will frame it like a degree in a doctor's or lawyer's office. I framed the one for my book, *The Passing of Mother Mary.*

3. If you want a faster route than manually mailing your registration, turn to the Internet and visit http://www.copyright.gov. Here, you can copyright your stories, poems, novellas, novels, songs, plays, screenplays, and almost any other kind of intellectual property. Don't go to any other site to do this; other sites will file the paperwork for you, but if you are concerned about the protection of your work and you are willing to invest the time to fill out the forms, you should go straight to the government copyright

website. For all Writers who really want to be published, this is the route to take. The other websites are nothing more than middlemen are; they will happily keep their ten- to thirty-dollar profit to register your book for you, but this is something you can—and should—do for yourself. You will receive the certification of registration in the mail in about six to eight weeks. That will be your trophy for all your efforts, worth a bottle of bubbly for the novice Writer! I had my glass of joy when I received the first certification of registration It was my Academy Award for personal achievement. You will be in a flood of tears as I was, so get Copyrighted!

Now that the Writer's Craft is mine by law, I can sue for plagiarism if the necessity arises. I once wondered, "Why do I have to protect my work once it is published? Who else can I trust to pursue my all of my efforts?" We have finished the Craft protected it, and now, we want to promote our Craft through Publishing.

This next step has a crack in it. We must climb this step very carefully, or we'll end up falling back down to Step 1. Have faith! We will continue to climb. This is our destiny, and we've already come too far to give up now.

The Writer in you will die when you put your pen down, put the paper away, and vow not to Read any more books! This is, of course, an abomination, but I was ready to do just that; I nearly fell off this next step. Now, I would rather learn from my mistakes and try again. I have failed so many tasks that failure was an option, but for the first time in my life, I wanted prove myself wrong. I wanted to learn that my Writer's Craft was nothing to be ashamed of and that I could take one more breath and leap without looking back.

This next step is called the Writer's Leap. You need faith, strength, and the willpower not to turn around. If you fall on this step, for God's

Sake, Get Back Up! You can cry, scream, and yell, but don't Stop your Craft!

At this point, you are no longer just a Writer. You are—or are about to be—a Published Author!

Take a deep breath. Hold the air inside. Concentrate. Blow your sigh out slowly. Now, step forward God bless you Writers... er, Authors!

ISBN and Publishing

I first tried the Subsidy Press publishing companies to learn the publishing business. I had to start somewhere, and many people have followed the same route. There's nothing wrong with it. You have to start somewhere and learn how to Publish your Craft by understanding the steps involved. This is the part where most people get scared, and I don't blame them. That leap is like leaping off a cliff, not knowing if the water below is shallow or deep. If you ever saw the movie *Titanic*, you will understand the fears the passengers had when they had to take that astounding leap. They didn't know if they would survive or be swallowed up by the freezing depths of the Antarctic waters. I'm scared just reading that part! But you have to take a good breath and hold it...then Leap!

The Subsidy will cost money. Doesn't everything in the Publishing business? Have a budget ready, a point I will expound on later. Do your research first. Now what is the difference between subsidy and vanity publishing Not much, really, but let me explain what I know.

I will explain the Vanity Press publishing first, mainly because you hear of these houses the most. Vanity presses are publishing or printing houses that print an Author's book at the sole cost of the Author. The overhead cost is more expensive than self-publishing, but the rights remain with the Author. You retain ownership of what you just produced, meaning your story. All sales and profit are yours, minus the charges for the editing, formatting into book form (typesetting), cover design, and the labor and materials involved in the printing process. One thing to remember is that vanity presses don't necessarily screen for quality and will publish almost any kind of work for which the Author has an open wallet, so if you Write quality work (which I hope you do), you may want to go another route.

What about Subsidy Publishing? Some people haven't heard of Subsidy presses, which are the same as Vanity press publishing, except that they may include the price of editing, distribution, and marketing in a lavish package or two. In other words, they dress it up like an extravagant evening gown or a tailored tuxedo. They might be able to tease you with their enticing packages the way you can tease a baby into cooperation with a lollipop. The downside is that the completed books are the property of the publishing house, which owns the ISBN. The Author receives a royalty, though the percentage is typically very low—far less than the authored serves.

Self-Publishing is what most novice Authors are investing in. With self-publishing, the Authors pay all costs for publishing their work. The Author has their say in who edits the work, who does the cover design, who prints the book, and who distributes the work to the markets. Authors who work with self-publishers do most of the marketing themselves. This way of publishing is cost-effective because the Author can find freelance or familiar editors at a lower rate, hire their own book cover designers, or even design their own cover, and use printers and distributors that offer better deals than the vanity or subsidy publishers do. Most importantly, the Author is the sole owner of the work—not only because they retain ownership of the rights, but also because they purchase their own ISBN for the work, and this is the best reward by far. The Author, in the end, reaps about 80 percent of sales after the contributed costs.

Many Writers believe Subsidy and Vanity Publishing is interchangeable, meaning they are similar in what they purport to do for the author. If you chose this route, that's your decision. I like to set sail in my own self-publishing boat. I like to control my Writer's Craft, and I set aside money to see my work sail across the seas of the world. I make time for the editors, cover designers, printer and distribution quotes, and above all, I arrange the marketing schemes that will be used to sell my books.

STEP 8: GET YOUR OWN ISBN/BARCODES

If your get your own ISBN number for your work, you own your Writer's Craft This number is yours, and no one can rob you of your sales. You become your own Publisher! It will cost between $125 and $250, but you'll probably pay a fraction of that same amount in editing costs, cover designing, distribution, and marketing.

If you have access to the Internet, I am strongly and, yes, seriously encouraging you to visit https://www.myidentifiers.com or http://isbn.org and pay for the single ISBN number or purchase a block of ISBN numbers. If you are going to Write a number of books, then the block of ten ISBNs is right for you. The ISBN number simply identifies the titles of your books and the publisher (which is you the Author) for ordering purposes. It must contain thirteen digits; therefore, if you find a site giving less than thirteen digits, these are bogus sites, and you need to beware of any "thieves in the night."

Subsidy/Vanity presses will assign or sell you one of their ISBNs at around ten to fifty dollars per book. They may tell you that you will "retain all rights," but this is unfortunately misleading. You are actually borrowing the ISBN. You don't own it, so a book retailer will go to the ISBN holder (Publisher to buy a bulk of your books, and you get only the contracted royalty, which you agreed upon in your signing of the contract.

If your book contract with your Subsidy press publisher ends, the ISBN for they had assigned to your book means your book will remain owned by them. In a case like this, your book is theirs, not yours, and you can't take it with you. I know this from experience.

My advice to you is that you own your own ISBN number. If you do, then even seventy years after your death, your children and perhaps their children can still profit from your Craft. There is nothing wrong with leaving your Writer's Craft to your future generations. I would love to have Charles Dickens or Shakespeare or even satiric poet Dante as my kin! I would show the talents of these Crafters with my head held high and pride crowning my chest as I boasted about them.

Lastly, don't forget the barcodes! Yes, this is necessary for your ISBN numbers. Retailers and booksellers scan these codes to give information to their computers, as to who is the publisher and how to order more books to sell. I suggest http://www.upccode.net to purchase these codes. Currently, this site charges eighty-nine dollars for one barcode. If you already have your ISBN number, you can have it placed on the barcodes, and printed on labels in quantities of ninety for about sixty dollars—a great deal! There are other sites to purchase these barcode(s). Research the Web for the best prices, and choose the site(s) that will best suit your needs.

Now go ahead and take the next step, and don't get exhausted yet! We've got to move forward. Take a deep breath and put one foot forward, then the next. We've come a long way, so just a few more steps, and we'll reach the top of our first mountain. Ready? No? Well, move on anyway! You'll thank me later for being so pushy!

PDF Files

What Is a PDF file?

PDF (Portable Document Format) is a file format created by Adobe Systems to enhance document exchange. These documents display resolution and can be read on electronic devices such the Sony eReader, Amazon Kindle, and Barnes and Noble Nook, the most innovative eBook devices. As the eBook market takes center stage on the book circuit, you, the author must keep up with the newest technology in order to sell your books. PDF files can contain graphics and/or text.

STEP 9: PDF FILES OF MANUSCRIPT AND COVER

If you are computer savvy at all, making a PDF is not difficult. Your first step is to Go to http://pdf-format.com and download the Adobe files. The instructions are self-explanatory.

Make a PDF file document of your soon-to-be Published book. You will need this to prevent any malicious changes, sent to the book printers, and load your book on some of the websites where eBooks are created.

Make a PDF file document of your book cover as well, especially if you want to send your book cover to a Publisher or an independent printer. You will also need this for eBook websites.

This is a must-have, and you must include PDF know-how and capability in your inventory of supplies needed to move your Writing forward. After this, we can take another Leap!

Printer/Distribution

You must now make the decision to send your work to a Publisher(s) or a Printer. If you choose publishing, you will pay the Publisher to complete the Publishing process, by having their printing companies print your book. If you choose the Printer method, you decide what printing company to use, and you can chose the quantity of books and the quality of paper and book cover(s) used.

You should also consider online printing services. There are some good online printers out there. http://www.*selfpublishing.com* is a good one, and they will walk you through the process. In the book business, you will always have to research and look for the best deals. If you find a Printing company you really like, stick with them. I look for digital printers that continually modify their technology to keep up with the times. Technology changes yearly, and you must keep up with the technological changes as well.

Who would have ever thought that in the writing world, we'd be using eBook, digital printing, and MP3 audio books? Like myself, we have to keep up with the times, okay Authors, move up another Step!

STEP 10: FIND A PRINTER/DISTRIBUTOR

Once you've got your Printer, you should search for a Distributor There are online Distribution companies that you should consider. Two of these are Lighting Source (http://www.lightningsource.com) and Ingram Company (http://www.ingrambook.com). You can also visit http://www.bookmasters.com for more information and suggestions. There are many others out there, so do your research and ask for plenty of quotes. If the Printer asks for $800 or more to print 100 books, that's a little costly and I would suggest you seriously consider searching for other printing outlets that are more reasonable.

Promoting and Marketing

This is one of the most difficult steps because while it is not hard to do, it requires a great deal of work. Promoting yourself and your work is an endless job. If you are a serious author, you will have to Promote your Craft for years. And why not? You are a Published Author now!

Social networking has blossomed into a rather large entity on the Internet. Facebook is the dominant site in today's market, Twitter comes second, and many others follow close behind. Creating pages, writing tweets, and blogging about your book on blog sites is a great—and usually free—way to keep your readers up-to-date and generate interest in your forthcoming novel. Just be careful, though, because it is easy to get carried away with social networking. While it will help you attract avid and interested readers, networking and marketing yourself on the Internet can take away some of your Writing time from your next novel. You need to find a way to invest ample time to both writing and networking.

You have finished a long-awaited project. Now Promote it! Why not? You've had your dream, and your vision is now in sight, and if you have Read this far, it is clear that you intend to take steps to ensure that your book is acknowledged not just by you, but also by your family, friends, and those who have supported your efforts. Of course, there are those avid readers whose interest you've now attracted as well.

I commend my Writers for Reading this far. For those of you who have followed me through these steps, as my grandmother once said, "You are greater than you think." Don't get lazy now! It's time to let everyone know how well you've done in Writing your dream novel...and Publishing it!

If you are computer savvy, then your creativity will lead you to produce your own promotional material. This is a inexpensive way of showing how unique you are. What promotional items would you want to display? The following are a few ideas that many authors use to promote themselves and illustrate that they take their Writer's Craft seriously. The promotional items I usually use to Promote myself.

STEP 11: PROMOTING YOURSELF

PRESS RELEASES. A Press Release about you or your book is one way to let your readers know that your book is finished and ready for purchase. This is a one-page letter that will be distributed to media outlets in your area as well as internationally. Make sure the title of your book and your name are spelled correctly. Give the first line a great opening. Don't forget to list the places of purchase, the ISBN number, and the Price. A quick synopsis should be included, but only in one sentence, no more than two. The

Press Release may be a little pricy, but it is well worth it.

ADVERTISE. Advertise on local media networks, in magazines and bookstores, and find venues to promote your book as well as your name. The more you advertise, the more you will be remembered. Start at a minimum and gradually increase your advertisement efforts. Internet advertisement is the most innovative way of reaching a large community of readers. Try Google, Yahoo, Bing, and other search engines to spread the word about your book.

PRESS KIT. Many marketers suggest a press or media kit, and I do too. It should include samples of your press releases, your author bio, your book title and a picture of it, sell sheets, business cards with pertinent information, bookmarks, and a favorite, professional-looking photo of you.

BUSINESS CARDS. These are a must. Pass them out to everyone, at every opportunity! Place your name, address, e-mail(s), website(s), book title(s), publishing company (optional), and any other pertinent information on the card. Be creative! I use www.vistaprint.com. They offer inexpensive and wonderful promotional items— such a personal favorite that I have bookmarked their site. They are very economical, and their promotional designs are very unique.

POSTCARDS. These are useful to mail out to libraries and booksellers. On these cards you have more freedom of design. Put your book design on the front, along with the name of your book, where to buy it, your email(s) and website(s), and any pertinent information. Again, I suggest http://www.vistaprint.com for great deals on postcards and other promotional materials.

BOOKMARKS. I really don't use these that much anymore because they are not as popular as some might think. I noticed on one book tour that bookmarks are not picked up as much as postcards. If you write children's books, this may he a hotter item, but for young adult and general adult fiction, they do not seem as popular. If you opt to have bookmarks printed, be just as creative as you are with your postcards.

FLYERS/POSTERS. Posting flyers is always a great way of letting your readers and the public know when and where your book signing(s) and book tour(s), seminar(s), and lecture(s) are happening, and where readers can view your website(s) and book trailer(s).

ORDER FORMS. Have these ready at your book fairs/signings just in case you run out of books. It can happen! You never know how well your books may sell. As a self-published author, I can only estimate how many books I should order to sell to my readers, but an actually bookseller (such as Barnes and Noble) can order your book in large quantities, even into the thousands, so they may not run out of your book so readily.

WEBSITE(S) AND BOOK TRAILER(S). With the Internet blasting into the twenty-first century, it would be foolish not to have a website(s) and book trailer(s) to help your readers find you.

Having too many websites and placing them on your promotional items will confuse your readers. They want your website(s) and book trailer(s) to be easily found. Why confuse your readers with complicated website(s) and book trailer(s)?

REMEMBER: K.I.S.S.—Keep It Simple Silly.

<u>MISCELLANEOUS ITEMS.</u> I like to display t-shirts with my book title(s) on them. I have pens, hats, cups, mouse pads, banners, posters, car magnets, bumper stickers, and so many other items. There are so many great publicity items out there. Promote Yourself!

Your sole purpose is to Promote you and your book—not just one time but also forever. You are an Author now, so keep your name and the name of your book always in the public's eye.

The first year I learned to promote myself, I went to bookstores and asked them to buy my book(s) on consignment, which is at a 40 percent discount. As you ask several bookstores to sell, you will see your clientele of booksellers increase.

Self-Publishers vs. Agents

After finishing writing, revising, proofreading, and taking care of all the necessary editing, you are ready to submit your book to an Agent. The Agent in the book industry prefers a completed manuscript, so be prepared for that. I suggest not only submit the manuscript, but other materials as well. Upon the Agent's requests, you should send them your author bio, website(s), book sales, flyer(s), and other material.

An Agent's job is to submit your work to a Publisher so it can make the book markets. To acquire an Agent is a painstaking task, but it is very necessary. Without an agent, you will have to do a lot of work yourself. If you are up to it, the long hours and extensive diligence and patience will eventually pay off. If you are Danielle Steel, Stephen King, or Robert Hicks, you've got an Agent and probably a good one.

Self-publishing is not new. Many Authors have done it for centuries. With the computer age, it is a lot easier. When you finish your manuscript and you want to Self-Publish the first thing after editing the work is to put it in PDF format, as we've already discussed. This will be required if you desire to publish on sites such as www.createspace.com or www.lulu.com. It is free on these sites to load up and create your book yourself, and you make all the decisions. I really like these sites because of their flexibility.

Self-Publishing is excellent for those who want to see their work displayed right away. Many Writers Self-Publish to get their work into the hands of their family and friends, to show off their private desires, talent, and dreams. Most Self-Published Writers publish their work for themselves first rather than for a particular book market. Self-accomplishment is their award.

The greatest trophy is that the author is picked up by an agent and their works make a wide market through a well-established Publisher.

Finding the right Agent is difficult, but it is possible with persistence. The place to start is the well-known book called *The Writer's Market,* an absolute must-have. When you get your copy of this book (a new edition comes out every year), you should go through it thoroughly. The foreword section should be read first if you are a novice. Be willing to spend some time in these informative pages.

Don't ever pay for an Agent; if they expect you to, it is likely a scam. A true Agent makes money when You make money, so you must choose wisely.

Learn how to create a query letter. This letter introduces you to your prospective agent, presents your works, and asks the Agent for their expertise in the book market to get publishers to view the work you so diligently worked on for months.

The Agent who picks you hopes you are not just a one-hit wonder. If you are just writing one book, an Agent will probably not jump to select your work to represent. Their business is just that—a business. Don't get mad at them! Many good agents really work hard to represent their clients, and they need to make a living as well as you do. The reality is, your Writing actually becomes a business, and you must comply with the business.

If you only want that one-book deal, self-publishing your book on self-publishing sites on the Internet is really for you. You wrote a book to satisfy yourself first, so why not have it Published, even if it is by the self-publishing method?

On the other hand, if you have many ideas or multiple books to be written, finding an Agent is your next step!

Time to climb again! Now that my book is complete and I know I will continue my venture of writing, I am looking for a good Agent. I know that my genre is fiction. I will not look in *The Writer's Market* for a nonfiction agent, textbook agent, religious book agent, or a self-help agent, etc. I have to focus on an agent within my genre.

If my story is, in fact, within my genre and is of interest to an open market, then my search for an Agent should not be difficult. Then saying it is one thing and doing it is another! Most of the good Agents, are in the major populated states, such as New York, California, Pennsylvania, Florida, Chicago, Illinois, and some in Washington, D.C. Many agents in England and Europe are willing to work with new authors from the States, and most agents are looking for that new Author, that new voice. Maybe that's You!

STEP 12: THE QUERY LETTER

The first thing an Agent will take an interest in is the query letter. This is what literary agents look for.

Several things should be included with your query. The manuscript should first have the title and author's name. The second page can be the title again, and then a short synopsis. The story synopsis should hook the agent. The following pages should be the first ten or fifteen pages of your manuscript. Use a common twelve-point font like Times Roman. If you use outlandish or silly fonts that are too large or difficult to read, your query and manuscript will most likely earn a quick pass to File 13—right into the shredder.

Your query letter should first tell the Agent who You are, what your intentions are, and what you want them to do. If you forget these things, they will forget you wrote them a letter.

Tell them what's so important about your book. What is your genre? What is your book about? How many pages is it, and who is the target audience?

If your query letter has been edited and is in a good, acceptable format, then you have hit the nail on the head. Good for you!

To determine who to send your query to, go back to your *Writer's Market,* your resource book. Take your time going through it, and once you've selected around 200 agents, you can begin sending out your queries. Don't expect a response right away. Also, you shouldn't be surprised if some agents request a partial or full manuscript; if they request your manuscript, send it to them, but don't send it unsolicited or unrequested. Again, don't stop writing if you haven't heard from an agent. If you are like me, you will start another writing project. A Writer Writes all the time. The Writer Craft is a never-ending adventure, so keep telling your stories.

Take rejection and move on to another agent. J.K. Rowling went to several agents and found the one agent who took that leap of faith with her and now, Hellooo, Harry Potter!

Query letters are usually a one-page, single-paced letter. You must grab the agent's immediate attention with a strong opening. Tell the Agent a little about your Writing skill. Most Agents want to evaluate your writing by Reading your synopsis and sample chapters.

Share Your Fame!

Now Share! Tell others who want to write how you did it. It won't be the Bible to the Writer's Craft, just Your guided experience.

STEPS 13: SHARE YOUR KNOWLEDGE

Yes! This is the Last Step! You have made it! Now Share your fame and success! But don't forget to hug and kiss yourself in the end!

The only thing I have to ask is that you do not become jealous and envious of other Writer's success. You will have your day, if not now, then someday. Keep hope alive! Continue to dream I lecture others, I motivate others, and I inspire others. Why? Why not? Others did it for me, so why not reciprocate? At book fairs, festivals, expos, and tours, I sell my books without thinking of the book sales of other authors. I know my limitations, and I have pushed the envelope just to see what would happen.

I will continue to Write stories mainly because this is the one so-called hobby that I love to do—a hobby that happened to became a reality. So if you are reading this book, well good for you. I know you will be a great success! You are now on the course to becoming a Published Writer!

I can't wait to see your work on the shelves or you can send a free copy to me. You, the Writer, have climbed a mountain that most people haven't dared to climb. You've visited a port that most sailors couldn't navigate on their own. You dared to dream a dream that most people couldn't fathom. And with any luck or ambition, you will continue to climb that mountain, sail that voyage, or dream that one never-ending dream of becoming a Writer.

Above all, I hope you illustrate The Writer's Craft in Your Novel!

SAMPLE BOOK BUDGET (UNDERLINE ESTIMATED) FOR
THE NOVICE OR FIRST-TIME WRITER

Your Time: Free!

Copyright: $35-$50

ISBN: $125 ($250-block of 10)

Barcodes: $29-$99($60-$1,000/blocks)

Editing: $100-$600 ($2.00/page)

Proofreading: $50-$200

Cover Design: $75-$200 per book

Printing Interior: $700-$1,200 per book

Book Orders: $60-$3,000 (60-300 books)

Marketing: $400-$3,000 per project

Press Releases: $60-$1,000 per release

Book Tours: $249-$350 per venue

Website(s): $120-$150 per year

TOOLS OF THE CRAFT I: VOCABULARY

Now that these 13 steps have been given to you as an insight to the Writer's Craft, I offer you these additional tools that can be used within the various steps. I continue to learn as I Write, and you must continue to climb new steps to perfect your Craft.

As I Write my stories, I continue to build an extensive vocabulary. So get a notebook! I use a composition book. Build your vocabulary by Reading other books and Writing what words they used to describe people, places, things, expressions, and actions. You can even record interesting dialogue said by the characters.

Words like menacing, audacity, lucrative, serenading, contorted, tousled, horde, mere, culpable, equidistant, skeptically, imprudent, methodically, fictitious, stealthily, obscured, bewilderment, acid, idly, excruciating, odious, attest, and plied are very useful and could enhance your storyline, but does the Reader know the meaning and usage of the words? If not, why use them? Try using the most common words, but keep your focus on storytelling. The reader wants your Craft, not your IQ. Please don't make your readers put the book down! A child would not understand Dante's *Inferno*, and neither do most avid readers. That book is usually Read by an above-average reader or intense intellectuals who like to enhance their repertoire of eccentric classical literature.

In my composition book, I usually Write the most unusual the descriptions, phrases, and dialogues that I have Read. I also like to Write how the writer made notes about fashion. I underlined their use of expressions and quotes. This is a good idea for the novice writer. I would use an easy book first, like *Family* by J. California Cooper, then slowly advance to a midgrade book like *Cane River* by Latina Tademy or *Harry Potter* by J.K. Rowling. The words from *Uncle Tom's Cabin* by Harriet Beecher-Stowe or *Jubilee* by Margret Walker might require a dictionary. I like learning new vocabulary words all the time, and now that you Write, so should you.

Some dialogue should be very dramatic. Readers want not only want to know *what* is said, but *how* it is said. You must find a way to describe your characters' statements in such a way that the reader can see the characters' expression as the comments are stated.

Words and Phrases like anxiously, replied quickly, responded with fear, asked hesitantly, said, yearning to know more, answered in a whisper, she interjected, he vented loudly, he echoed, he hissed, she scowled angrily, the child muttered, the old man groaned will inform the reader what the character is feeling or sometimes thinking. Be poetic!

I also try to use metaphors or similes to make my tale interesting. Metaphors and Similes describe objects by comparing them in a poetic way. Similes use the words "like" or "as," while Metaphors do not. Samples of Similes are: beautiful as a swan; tall as a tree; skinny like a twig' dumb as a dog (yet I do hold this to be totally true since my dog was smart as a whip); gentle as a puppy; and many others. The Metaphor is at times worded with difficulty. For instance: he had rusty knees; she had nerves of steel; he had an iron heart; the boy had a lion's roar; the boxer had a glass jaw; and many, many more. Try *The Bibliophiles Dictionary*, one of my must-haves. Use Metaphors and Similes in your Craft, it will always be part of Creativity, and that's what you want your readers to enjoy.

TOOLS OF THE CRAFT II: IMAGINATION

Many writers are inspired with ideas for stories when they watch movies. A newscaster may even put a wild Idea in your head on the evening news, whether it is a story about a kidnapping, rape, murder, robbery, assault, or some other interesting tale. As the days go by, we gather more information and then our imagination goes wilder. Thus, we create our stories Let's look at some examples of some stories I'm working on:

Two women are separated at birth, then are suddenly are reconnected by a runaway fugitive. The fugitive has information about their parents and will only divulge the information if they will clear his name from a crime he didn't commit, since one is a lawyer and the other is a detective.

A man hated his girlfriend because she gave him an ultimatum to get a job or get out of her house. He suddenly snapped and attempted to kill her and her child and then shot himself. What if she found out how crazy he was and then hired a bodyguard to protect her and her kid, but fell in love with him, only to find out he is her boyfriend's stepbrother and he is just as mental.

A senator had a affair, and his mistress is now pregnant, so she slams him in the media, but after their last meeting on a train ride, which collides and kills them both, the senator's wife chooses to raise the mistress's child since she is barren.

A rich guy marries a divorcee from New York who is below his financial social status and must deal with society or run from it and live where they can be accepted but finds that racism continues to engulf every avenue of society and has not been suppressed as he thought.

A supermodel earns her fame all too suddenly and has to learn to cope with the media following her day and night. To escape, she poses as a man in rags, only to be robbed and lose her memory of her past life.

A woman works her way to a financial institution using her looks but is in peril when she finds out that the accounting firm is laundering money for drug cartels in Colombia and with the money they help finance wars in the Middle East. How does she reveal the truth to save her life?

A serial killer who once worked for a scientific corporation begins a killing rampage in a small nearby town. He puts a chemical in the town water supply and poisons as many people as he can before a FBI agent chases up with him. He has to get the antidote from the killer to save his own child.

A Catholic priest helps a child named Brownlow run away from her evil Aunt Mary Catherine before she finds out that the child has a million-dollar inheritance awaiting her when she turns eighteen. As the aunt goes after Brownlow, she involves her father, who is released for prison after many years of prosecution for the murder of her grandmother. Can Investigator Phillip Talley find Brownlow before it's too late?

So how is your imagination? Can you get yourself to look at the newscasts and let your mind run wild? That's what some Writers do, and that's what's called imagination.

TOOL OF THE CRAFT III: BOOK SET-UP PAGES

Page 1: Title Page-<u>ALWAYS ON ODD PAGE</u>

-Title of your book (+ Sub Title)

-Author(s)

-Publisher(s)

-Location of Publisher(s)

Sample

The Writing Craft:

My 13 Steps

By DC Brownlow

Conant Gardens Publishing

Detroit, MI 48212

Page 2: Copyright Page-<u>AFTER TITLE PAGE</u>

The Writing Craft: My 13 Steps -**Title**

By DC Brownlow -**Author**

Copyright © 2011 BY Christina 'DC Brownlow' Reyes
All rights reserved. **–Copyright year**

No part of this book may be reproduced, stored in a retrieval system, or transmitted by any means without the written permission of the author. - **Disclaimer**

Printed in the United States of America.
This book is printed on acid-free paper – **Declaration (Optional)**

ISBN 978-0-9828603-0-4- **ISBN Number**

CONANT GARDENS PUBLISHING CO. – **Publishing Co.**

Detroit Michigan 48212- **Location**
United States

<u>www.conantgardens.com</u> –**Email Contact**

Page 3: Dedication Page –For your supporters

ALWAYS ON ODD PAGE #

Dedication

This book is dedicated to all those who find writing a difficult task and yearn for an easier way to expose their writing craft.

DON'T SAY IT ANYMORE...JUST DO IT!

Page:

1. **Blank Page -Insert Blank Page**

2. **Title Page -again for creativity**

3. **Blank Page -Insert Blank Page**

Page 7:   Contents or Beginning Chapter –ALWAYS ON ODD PAGE

THE NEVER, NEVER, NEVERS!

1. **Never** rush your manuscript. Let your story write itself.

2. **Never** publish without a professional editor.

3. **Never** let your family and friends proofread your work; use an avid reader that does not know you.

4. **Never** sign a contract without seeking legal advice first.

5. **Never** over-order your books; they just will collect dust. Sell your first 90, then order 150 on the second order. If you sell those during your book tours, you can determine how much to order and when.

6. **Never** stop networking and marketing your book(s).

7. **Never** stop querying for agents if self-publishing.

8. **Never** sell a book at a book tour without signing it.

9. **Never** stop selling yourself as a writer/author.

AND NEVER, NEVER, NEVER, STOP SHARING YOUR WRITER'S CRAFT WITH OTHERS!

WRITING REFERENCES

On Writing by Stephen King

Writing a Novel by John Blaine

Publish Basics by Johnson/Pramschufer

Writing to Tell a Story by Globe Fearon

The Elements of Style by E.B. White

The Passing of Mother Mary by Christina
Reyes

Their Eyes Watching God by Zora Hurston

Write to Learn by Donald M. Murray

The Writer's Market by Writer's Digest Books

Bibliophiles Dictionary by Peter Miles Westly

MY FAVORITE NOVELS

Reading classic novels helps writers to develop an understanding of the Writer's Craft. In order to Write well, you have to Read novels that are well written. I enjoyed these stories and know you will too.

Family by J. California Cooper

Kindred by Octavia Butler

The Color Purple by Alice Walker

Jubilee by Margret Walker

The Widow of the South by Robert Hicks

The Guns of the South by Harry Turtledove

The Crystal Cave by Mary Stewart

Middle Passage by Charles Johnson

Jane Eyre by Charlotte Bronte

WEBSITE RESOURCES

http://www.sfwa.org   http://www.bookmasters.com

http://www.isbn.org   http://www.book-hub.com

http://www.selfpublishing.com   http://www.ehow.com

http://www.copyright.gov   http://www.upccode.net

http://www.createspace.com

http://www.smashwords.com

http://www.aprexreviews.com

http://www.facebook.com

http://www.twitter.com

http://www.amazon.com

http://www.wordclay.com

http://www.lulu.com/content

http://www.linkedin.com

http://www.vistaprint.com

http://www.pdf-format.com

http://www.lightningsource.com

http://www.ingrambook.com

http://www.atlasbooks.com

QUERY LETTERS SAMPLE FORMAT

The purpose of a fiction proposal is to get Agents interested so they will to Read your complete manuscript. Your fiction proposal should be a single Microsoft Word document or Adobe Acrobat PDF file that includes:

A. Proposal Cover Page

This includes the title, author's name, physical address, email address, the genre of your novel (romance, mystery, Civil War, WWII historical, general fiction, etc.), and the length (word count).

B. "Sell Sheet"

You will need a one-page overview that captures the flavor of your novel: think a big back cover and presents its setting, major themes, and historical era. This is an important part of your proposal, so take your time to do it well.

C. Bio

Write about your writing experience, prior publishing history, education, and relevant achievements. These days, publishers look as closely at authors as they do at manuscripts.

Don't be modest. Include any writing-related awards you have won.

D. Story (Synopsis)

Write a three-to five-page synopsis of your story. The goal of a synopsis is to convince the reader that you have crafted a complete and compelling story, worthy of their time.

E. First 30 Pages

Send the first 30 pages of your novel. Use a simple page format, with approximately one-inch margins on the top, bottom, and sides. Select a standard font, like 12-point Times New Roman, double-spaced. Remember don't justify right-hand margins.

F. Market Analysis

Discuss your audience and your ability, if any, to sell books at speaking engagements, seminars, conferences, and other events. List other novels published within the past five years that are similar to your proposed work. Tell us why your novel is more compelling.

G. Author Marketing

Set up a website for your book, create and purchase promotional materials, and arrange your own book signings, or attend writers' conferences. Think creatively when you come up with marketing ideas, and indicate if you will be able to get a well-known writer to endorse your book.

H. History of the Manuscript

Tell if you submitted the manuscript to editors and/or publishers by yourself. Writers often meet editors at writers' conferences and other events and come away with opportunities to make direct submissions.

A note about first novels: it usually doesn't make sense for a first-time novelist to develop a proposal until the manuscript is complete. Few mainstream publishers will buy a first novel without a finished manuscript.

ABOUT THE AUTHOR

Christina Reyes (DC Brownlow)

     Christina E. Reyes began writing at age fourteen, due greatly to the constant encouragement of her grandmother, Tinnie Maude Talley, who encouraged her to pursue eloquence and excellence in speaking and writing in spite of difficult obstacles. Christina enjoys writing stories based on philosophical views, humorous tales, and family-oriented novels that consist of emotional and personal experiences.

     Christina Reyes currently resides in a prominent area of Detroit, Michigan known as Conant Gardens. Christina looks forward to writing more stories that will be enjoyed by readers worldwide.

     Other books by Christina Reyes:

     **The Passing of Mother Mary

     **From Michigan Maine to Harvard

Author's contact information:

     www.conantgardens.com

     dcbrownlow@gmail.com

www.ingramcontent.com/pod-product-compliance
Lightning Source LLC
Chambersburg PA
CBHW060252050426
42448CB00009B/1617